CHALLENGE GAME

BY **LEARN WITH FUN EDITIONS**

LEARN WITH FUN EDITIONS is pleased to publish this amazing book that will let you discover the most worldwide famous monuments and places in the world.

With this book you will discover and learn with fun some of the most popular places and monuments.

You can challenge yourself or by groups by trying to guess the name of the monuments before checking the answers at the end of the book.

Every good answer is 1 point and the one who find the most correct answers will win the game.

THE ONLY
THING YOU
HAVE TO DO IS
TO OPEN YOUR
EYES
AND
HAVE FUN

1.

2.

3.

4.

5.

6.

7.

8.

9.

10.

11.

12.

13.

14.

15.

16.

17.

18.

19.

20.

21.

22.

23.

24.

25.

26.

27.

28.

29.

30.

31.

32.

33.

34.

35.

36.

37.

38.

39.

40.

41.

42.

43.

44.

45.

46.

47.

48.

49.

50.

51.

52.

53.

54.

55.

56.

57.

58.

59.

60.

61.

62.

63.

64.

65.

66.

67.

68.

69.

70.

71.

72.

73.

74.

75.

76.

77.

78.

79.

80.

81.

82.

83.

84.

85.

86.

87.

88.

89.

90.

91.

92.

93.

94.

95.

96.

97.

98.

99.

100.

101.

102.

103.

104.

105.

106.

107.

108.

109.

110.

111.

112.

113.

114.

115.

116.

117.

118.

119.

120.

ANSWERS

1-Statue of Liberty
2-Eiffel Tower
3-Big Ben
4-Leaning Tower of Pisa
5-Colosseum
6-Golden Gate Bridge
7-Notre Dame
8-Tokyo Tower
9-London Eye
10-St. Peter's Basilica
11-Sagrada Familia
12-Great Wall of China
13-Sydney Opera House
14-St. Basil's Cathedral
15-Arc de Triomphe
16-Berlin Wall
17-Stonehenge
18-Kilimanjaro
19-Uluru-Ayers Rock
20-Taj Mahal
21-Pyramids of Giza
22-The Great Sphinx
23-Tower Bridge
24-The forbidden City, China
25-Mont Everest
26-Capitol Hill
27-Brooklyn Bridge
28-Burj Al Arab Hotel
29-Acropolis, Greece
30-Trevi Fountain
31-St. Mark's Basilica & Campanile
32-Times Square
33-The White House
34-Louvre Museum
35-Buckingham Palace
36-Versailles

37-Neuschwanstein Castle
38-Matterhorn
39-Pompeii
40-Florence Cathedral
41-Edinburgh Castle
42-Machu Picchu
43-Christ the Redeemer- Rio De Janeiro,Brazil
44-CN Tower
45-The Grand Canyon
46-Niagara Falls
47-Burj Khalifa
48-Tower of London
49-Madrid Palace
50-Mont St. Michel, France
51-Las Vegas
52-Petronas Twin towers
53-Windsor Castle
54-Sacre Coeur, Paris
55-St. Paul's Cathedral
56-Central Park
57-Mount Rushmore
58-Mount Fuji
59-Rialto Bridge
60-Arena Di Verona
61-Pace Needle
62-Westminster Abbey
63-Rock of Gibraltar
64-Alcatraz
65-White Cliffs of Dover
66-Iguazu National Park, Argentina
67-Washington monuments
68-The Shard
69-The Gherkin
70-Moai
71-Temple of Luxor
72-Brandenburg Gate,Berlin

73-Cologne Cathedral
74-Pentagon
75-Vesuvio
76-Mayan Pyramids of Chichen Itza
77-Cloud Gate, Chicago
78-Angkor Wat, Cambodia
79-Victoria Falls
80-Terracotta Warriors
81-Potala Palace, Lhasa
82-Petra
83-Yellostone National Park
84-Hagia Sophia
85-Oriental Pearl Tower
86-Nyhavn
87-Ponte Vecchio
88-Al Aqsa Mosque, Palestine
89-The Dome of the Rock, Palestine
90-Kaaba in Mecca
91-Sydney Harbor Bridge
92-Sistine Chapel
93-Spanish Steps
94-Makkah Royal Clock Tower Hotel, Mecca, Saudi Arabia
95-Hassan II mosque
96-Berlin Cathedral
97-Helsinki Cathedral
98-Medina Mosque
99-Bath, England
100-Soissons Cathedral, Soissons (France)
101-Saint Jean des vignes, Soissons (France)
102-Cayan Tower, Dubai
103-Atlantis The Palm, Dubai
104-Alhambra
105-Papel Palace, Avignon
106-Pond du Garre
107-Festung Hohensalzburg
108-Bran Castle

109-Prague Castle
110-Piazza Del Campo, Siena
111-Portofino
112-Atomium, Brussels
113-Guggenheim Museum (Bilbao)
114-Death Valley
115-Winter Palace
116-Amalienborg Palace
117-Kremlin
118-Blue Mosque, Istanbul
119-Hercules cave morocco
120-Trafalgar Square